Would You Fly What You Fix?

A Technician's Handbook

By

Mark L. Dzierzbicki

With

Tom Kaminski

Cover Work by
Nicole Hampton

Would You Fly What You Fix?

Special thanks to Neil Hayes for his advice during the writing of this book.

Would You Fly What You Fix?

Table of Contents

Would You Fly What You Fix?

Would You Fly What You Fix?

Author's Note

Talent and Desire – Your Handshake to Society

Why should you read this book? Why should you care about your work?

Because it's your handshake to society and your profession, that's why. Call it your legacy and your reputation.

Will your handshake be firm, showing resolve and confidence? Or will it be a weak handshake, lacking energy and strength?

If you want to play piano like Duke Ellington, you have to care about your practice and performance. Parents, teachers and mentors can all provide direction and support that can nurture talent. The effort and dedication, though, reside in the musician.

Talent, desire, and caring are the critical gears that drive success. Technicians we trust, anyone who picks up a tool to make a repair, and anyone who has a job to complete, should carry that same pride in their work.

This book is for those dedicated workers.

Would You Fly What You Fix?

Foreword

He's in Trouble Now...

The drop cloth on the floor was covered with parts, all neatly arranged. There were gears, chains, relays, a drum (photoreceptor), a developer housing (with 30 lbs. of developer), and other countless other parts that I had no name for. The copier, when assembled, weighed about 2,000 lbs., but most of that was now on the floor. There was no way this was going back together.

I was home from college and accepted an invitation from Mark to go to work with him on a Saturday. The customer's office was closed, and there were no employees around. The security guard let us in, and we rode the elevator to the office, where we entered the copier room. This copier had been in place awhile, had run a lot of copies, and needed to be overhauled, on-site. It was a big job and doing it on Saturday meant that the customer wouldn't lose working time on the copier.

Parts had been ordered and delivered. Now, after about two hours, the insides of the machine were spread out before us on the floor.

Would You Fly What You Fix?

I've known Mark since 3rd grade and had seen him working on cars. Tune-ups, brake jobs, and rebuilding engines. I'd noticed that appearances were always casual, but the work was always serious. Cars have to start, and sometimes, more importantly, they had to stop. That's why the repairs were serious. As a relatively non-technical guy, I asked questions, and Mark often knew the answers because he was always interested in how, and why, things work.

Still, here we were, downtown in some office, with their copier on the floor, in pieces.

After lunch, the re-assembly began. Three and a half hours later, the machine was back together. It was running and chugging along, working perfectly. Chugging is the right word, too, because there was a pneumatic paper feed system that gave these machines a distinct sound. Good techs listen to their machine, with subsystems working and sounding off in the correct order. The paper feed was flawless, and copy quality was good. (Copy quality was never excellent with that old developer and cascade development system.) It operated flawlessly, and I was more than slightly impressed.

Would You Fly What You Fix?

Mark has been making things work for quite a while. He's worked for big and small companies. He's an entrepreneur, a manager, and a business owner. He fixes cars, equipment, employees, customers, and businesses. He's always good company. He shares his insights into business, has some good laughs along the way, and lots of stories about fixing things.

Tom Kaminski

Would You Fly What You Fix?

Chapter 1

Would You Fly What You Fix?

How reliable are your repairs? Would you get into a helicopter that you just repaired?

My title —*Would You Fly What You Fix?*—was not chosen by accident.

I had met a helicopter mechanic who did fly what he fixed. He told me a story about flying in a helicopter he had just serviced, and was on-board when the copter had a mechanical failure and made a crash landing. There were no physical injuries, but he admitted to being more than a bit shaken by the experience. An investigation revealed that he missed an adjustment that caused the crash.

"I don't think I ever picked up a wrench again without remembering it," he told me. "And I know that falling out of the sky in something that I had "fixed" made me a better mechanic." Without doubt, the experience left an indelible mark on the soul of his mechanical spirit.

Having the education, talent and correct tools must be part of the aviation technician's basic

Would You Fly What You Fix?

requirements for the work day. But the people who fix things that fly must have a special, daily desire to make sure everything is fixed to a degree of reliability that would allow that technician to put him, or others, 30,000 feet in the air without concern.

I held a service meeting many years ago where I told the story of that helicopter mechanic. This was a life-changing event for him, and I wanted others to understand the high stakes that some technicians work with. I often end many of my service meetings and seminars with the challenge: "Would *you* fly what you fix"?

Imagine it's Christmas Eve, and you're about to assemble a bicycle as a present for your daughter. Tools are out, the box is opened, and you find that the wrong instructions were packaged with the bike. Or, the instructions are indecipherable because they were written as an afterthought.

This surely brings us to a philosophical question, when it comes to the ethics of repair, should there be a difference between an airplane and a bike? Can we fix that bike with the same discipline we'd use for an airplane? If so, what can we do to prevent these lapses?

Would You Fly What You Fix?

Think about what that helicopter mechanic learned. Consider the image of pilots and passengers falling out of the sky because of a mechanical error. That mechanic wound up with a newfound sense of excitement and enthusiasm about performing outstanding repair work.

It is with this challenge in mind, uplifting, to be sure, but also rooted in a healthy measure of enlightened self-interest that I want to share with you the philosophy of "Would You Fly What You Fix."

You'll find a renewed commitment to doing the job right, whatever the job is. You'll gain clarity and confidence, and find a clear path to the success you want and deserve. Just as important, you'll learn how to instill this in the people you work with, and the young, upcoming fixers of things. People, whether customers or family, depend on us, the service technicians, to repair with care the first time. Whether it's a copier, sprinkler system, Christmas gift or an airplane.

Chapter 2

The True Fixer

Why we need service repair people and the story of the first technician.

Technology failures began soon after humans first made something work. This created the new business of "repair" followed by language somewhat unique to the repair industry. Terms like "intermittent failure" and "hard failure" probably came first. This might have been followed by simple technical terms like: tolerances, torque, adjust, and of course, *No Problem Found*. More terminology followed. Stripped! Bent! Cheap aftermarket parts. Shorted, seized, and unserviceable.

In the beginning, it might have started something like this. Caveman Bob, (the first customer) realized that he needed Caveman Bill to fix something.

"Hey-We got stuff that's broke."

Caveman Bill had an ability to "fix" broken things and he became the first technician. Even in those days, I'm sure it didn't take the customers too

Would You Fly What You Fix?

long to question the serviceman's methods…or the service charges.

At some point in history, someone had the need to call a technician. There was a problem that needed more skill than the typical caveman possessed. He needed someone with the ability to correct an incorrect something or other.

It's important to note that desire, skill, and insight must have started out back then, too. These things go hand in hand when referring to the "True Fixer." One of my favorite sayings is, "Find out what you do well, and find out what makes you happy…and if God is smiling on you, they will both be the same thing." That's often the case for a True Fixer, even back then.

The True Fixer has always been faced with frustrating complications that are too much for their capabilities to fix. These challenges are driven by any number of issues common to the service business. Poor parts support, poor support from management, frustration, poor engineering, or just too much broken stuff waiting to be fixed. More importantly, too many customers waiting for problems to be resolved. As a True Fixer, these are lapses that must be overcome, and are understood to be temporary setbacks. There could have been a

Would You Fly What You Fix?

humorous side to all this evolution. Maybe the first "fail safe" device was invented by someone who was chased around a room by his new invention. With spectators watching, he may have realized the need for what we now call a "dead man" switch.

I've been taking things apart to find out how they work since I was a boy. Somewhere along the line, I had to, maybe wanted to, put things back together and make them work again. I've come to believe that people with true mechanical skills and the desire to fix broken things are born, not made. However, in my opinion, *great technicians*, are made, and not born.

At the risk of sounding like a proud papa, I noticed, early-on, an inherent mechanical aptitude in both my daughter and son. I introduced them to tools, and how broken things can be fixed. At the age of two, my son came in the room holding a broken toy. It was one of those ducks that waddle on the end of a stick that you push. He looked at me, called out "Daya," and motioned that I should follow him to the garage.

This is where we fixed things. He knew! This is where we repaired a full size satellite dish gearbox. This is where we later disassembled a 1969

Would You Fly What You Fix?

GTO for restoration. This is the place we built a go-cart from junk yard stuff. This is where he developed his sense of how to gain mechanical advantage. Most of all, this is the place he learned to improvise, and even do a bit of "jerry rigging." I was even more proud when the kids in the neighborhood began looking for him whenever their bikes and scooters needed repairs.

My daughter first showed her skills while I was assembling some metal shelving. She was about 3 years old when she saw what I was doing and asked to help. I didn't need to explain how to thread the nut onto the bolt! She learned from observation. It was also interesting to see that she understood that some of the areas to work in were inconvenient. Instead of saying "I can't get at that nut", she became resourceful. She simply repositioned herself for a better view of the problem and could now make her adjustment.

So, you can understand why I am a true believer that people are born with these basic skills. Parents, teachers, and mentors can help identify these basic skills.

Would You Fly What You Fix?

Their guidance and direction is what helps develop those skills. This is where the True Fixers are forged. This book will speak to them.

Chapter 3

What was that about Newton?

Understanding components, systems, their purpose and why over-confidence develops poor work habits.

A good friend once told me that you don't get in an airplane and say..."Screw Newton." His language was much more colorful. In other words, technicians must be grounded in the knowledge of their product, the purpose of that product, and the theory of how it works. One must have an understanding of how each component or system works in order to understand why, sometimes, it no longer does.

I developed my skills, and made my living, through many years of troubleshooting and repairing things. I was not always the best employee, nor was I always the best technician. But when I decided to move to the next level, I knew what I had to change. Over time, I made changes in the way I thought and worked. I realized that my

Would You Fly What You Fix?

work was important and that my customers depended on me to fix their problems. It wasn't just a machine being repaired, I was making it possible for my customer to complete his work and earn his pay. Happy customers meant that I would have a job and get paid for my work, too.

Having fixed things for the last forty-plus years, I've had the pleasure and benefit of being around some of the best technicians on the planet. I've also had the opportunity to see undisciplined repairmen and observe some of the least skilled people employed by any industry. I learned that it's important to have confidence in yourself, but always remember that a "spanking" can be right around the corner, at your next service call. Confidence is fine, but overconfidence can lead to sloppiness, shortcuts, and ultimately, poor work habits that result in inferior repairs. The "spanking" is the callback and an unhappy customer, for a problem that was missed in troubleshooting.

Having a false sense of confidence will make you your own worst enemy as a service person. The best technicians know that there's always something to learn and that's one of the reasons good service people like the job. Technicians often see new and

Would You Fly What You Fix?

challenging problems every day. Good service people have the discipline that drives them to head back to the service vehicle in the winter, or walk to the parts depot two blocks away to get the parts needed to finish the job correctly.

The same discipline applies to making the effort required to have the right tools or equipment to do the job properly. You need to tell yourself, on a Friday afternoon when you're waiting for the weekend to start, that you are not going to accept "good enough." Time must be taken to troubleshoot thoroughly, even when though a party may start without you.

I mentioned the word "employee" along with being a technician. Being a good employee is a big part of being a complete technician. Aside from adhering to company policies and the basics like showing up every day, and on time, there are important duties and responsibilities that are unique to the profession of service and repair. For example:

1. *Interaction with customers is almost always part of the job.*
2. *Technicians must often provide reports on the performance of new products or parts.*

(2. Cont'd) Maintaining an effective parts and tool inventory is essential in getting the job complete.

3. *Communicating with other technicians regarding new problems or solutions, inferior parts, sharing alternative repairs that can strengthen the entire service department.*

4. *Ethics is an increasingly important aspect of the job for professional technicians. Learn to protect the company, the product, and yourself. More on that in the next chapter.*

Chapter 4

Protect and Defend

How to protect the company and your job, and being a pro while you're doing it.

"To protect and defend", sounds like an episode of a police TV show. Just saying it out loud sounds like it may even have some felonious undertones. Neither is true.

This was a phrase regularly used quite a while ago in some parts of corporate America. Although I teach this philosophy to my employees today, I haven't heard much about it recently. It refers to the general approach that a field service representative or any employee should take when dealing with customers. When speaking to customers, be brief in your comments and avoid making negative remarks.

This book talks about doing things the right way, but let's face it; things don't always go that way. Here are some examples:

Would You Fly What You Fix?

You arrive at the service call and the irate customer immediately starts loudly complaining about how long they waited for service. The incorrect response is telling the customer that you had to drive 50 miles because the new dispatcher goofed up your whole schedule today.

The professional way to handle this situation is to make a simple but sincere apology for any inconveniences that the delay may have caused. Ask about the problem they're having, and listen intently. Finish that off with "I'm going to get right on it". If the customer demands more of a response, advise them that after you've solved their problem, you will contact your supervisor. Your goal is to make sure this doesn't happen again, and you want the customer to understand that you are looking out for their best interests.

Never make promises about reimbursements or any other compensation. Leave that to management. Speak to your manager about potential compensation, and the attitude of the customer when you left. Were they still irate, or were they satisfied with the work performed. A simple follow up call from a manager might help ease customer concerns. As a company representative, and a team player, you can be part

Would You Fly What You Fix?

of long lasting solutions. Don't be offended if your idea is not used. Management might have history or contractual obligations with the customer that will guide their decision.

Another scenario is when the technician, while troubleshooting, sees inherent design flaws or poor craftsmanship. That technician may fully understand proper design, and always execute best repair practices, but he must be cautious in framing his comments to the customer about their system.

In this instance the tech might say, "Obviously, whoever installed the system was incompetent." But what if the customer's recently deceased father designed and installed the system. Ouch!

Or, not as dramatic, the work may have been done by a friend that is no longer in business. There are a number of inappropriate responses and each has the potential for bringing the worst and most awkward response.

Here's another one: The tech has just finished correcting a problem and says that the last tech missed the problem entirely. The customer says that all the problems are from a technician at YOUR company, and has been improperly servicing it all along. This is the "Oops" moment, where the

Would You Fly What You Fix?

technician becomes silent and stares at the customer with a blank expression.

Sometimes, you have the "Eureka!" moment when you solve a problem that the previous company and technician completely missed. After explaining your diagnosis to the customer, you may be asked how it got that way, and I'm telling you to be careful.

After you have qualified, beyond a shadow of a doubt, that it was your competition that did the lousy work, I suggest that some business ethics and tact should be incorporated into your answer. You have no obligation to apologize or defend your competition's actions. Simply state that "I made these two adjustments…" By this time, the customer usually will volunteer that it was your competition that was there last. Let the customer read between the lines to understand who was at fault.

I believe that the best finish to the whole dialogue is "Well, it's not the first time I've seen this. Let me show you what I did to make it right." And then make damn sure you made it right. Let them know that it's fixed and that you should be their vendor from now on.

Consider this result when the previous technician was one of your own. This is an

Would You Fly What You Fix?

uncomfortable moment for any tech. It's important to remember that the technician in question may go back to this account someday. You may know that he's competent and that this does not represent his good efforts and regular performance.

This is walking on eggshells time. I've been in this situation myself and I handled it by analyzing the whole situation first. Is the Customer standing in front of me? Does the customer have a mechanical aptitude similar to mine? How well do I know this customer? The answer to these questions will vary from situation to situation.

In the first instance, I brought the customer over to the equipment that I had just finished repairing. I asked "Do you know Bob, the tech that was here the last time"? (I already knew that the customer knew and liked Bob.) She said "Oh yes, he's a nice guy and he's been fixing our machine for years". I mentioned that he is a good guy, but that I'm going to give him hell at lunch because it looks like he left this screw a little loose and that was the whole problem. She chuckled and told me to say hello when I see him. Mission accomplished. The customer was happy and I preserved the reputation of the technician.

Would You Fly What You Fix?

On another occasion I was following a technician that was on probation, and his work showed why he had earned that status. Even so, I asked the customer, who was standing there, to give me a few minutes to check things out. I could see immediately what the problem was. As soon as she left, I made the correct repair and checked other systems thoroughly. I reported to her that I wasn't sure exactly how the component came loose, but assured her that I've seen it before, and I've just corrected it so it doesn't happen again.

As I said earlier, things don't always go right. We all know that perfection is elusive and includes your company and fellow employees. The company may have policies and procedures that you don't agree with. Sharing that disagreement with the customer is completely unnecessary.

Following technicians that do substandard work does not make a fun day, especially if you're underpaid and not appreciated by your boss. However, neither of these things should be shared with your customer. Even if you disagree with me, you must admit that sharing your problems with the customer will solve absolutely nothing.

Working for a big corporation that sometimes finds itself in the news can also be a

challenge at the job site. Some customers might try to irritate you about things they've read, or try to uncover more information about some alleged wrongdoing. I've found that the best way to deflect those questions is to say, with a genuine smile, "I don't really pay attention to any of that. So, tell me, what were the symptoms of your equipment's problem?" You, single-handedly, can play a role in preventing further damage to your company by practicing a "protect and defend" personal policy. Show the customer that your company employs real talent. You!

Realize that although there may be real problems with your company, there is no benefit gained by participating in the "pile on". Like it or not, word does get around in each industry. You don't want to have the reputation for being openly ready to magnify problems of any one person or your own company.

Obviously, scenarios that involve a customer threatening you physically should be handled with common sense. Company policy and your professionalism will dictate how you should act in those rare instances.

Chapter 5

With Customers and Fixing Things

Working with the customers and a story about fireballs in the customer's office.

One time, returning from a vacation, I met with my field service manager for a kind of debriefing, getting updated on events during my absence. He asked, tongue-in-cheek, if I was glad to be back. I said, in all sincerity, that during my train ride to work, I was wondering what my first call would be. I remember saying that I was looking forward to that first problem.

I'll never forget the look on his face. You could see a couple of possible reactions he was having. Was I being sarcastic with him and he wasn't getting the joke? Or, was I truly honest and just an oddball person. Really...I loved that job. Most of the time.

Many of my customers were also my friends. I looked forward to going back into my accounts, seeing everybody and fixing their equipment

24

Would You Fly What You Fix?

problems. When I think back about it, they also enjoyed seeing me back on the job.

I was fortunate to have been trained by a major corporation like Xerox®, particularly because of the product line I serviced. In today's times it is becoming less common for machines to have such diverse use of components.

My teammates and I regularly used micrometers, special jigs, pyrometers, pressure and vacuum gauges and, of course, a multi-meter. We troubleshot mechanical systems that consisted of chains, pulleys, jack screws, gear trains, cam followers, and more. Even more typical of the era was the use of mechanical relays, limit switches, vacuum tubes and circuit boards that were the size of my hand that performed probably 1/10000 of what the same size piece of phenolic material does today.

Certainly, there is equipment out there today that requires a diverse knowledge of mechanics and electronics and I applaud the service people who tackle those mechanical wonders. (I'm also a bit jealous that I'm not fixing it with them.)

Would You Fly What You Fix?

This story is a particularly good example of what's called "Murphy's Law". A service tech I knew was repairing a copy machine at a school. He told the story something like this: A large subsection of the machine had to be removed to provide access to another component. This, in turn, exposed a set of electrical components and connections. In this situation, caution must be exercised, because there's a strong possibility of getting zapped by electricity. What makes this story interesting is that electrocution, the obvious punch line, was not the outcome. Before removing that large component, he had cleaned another part that required the use of a cotton material and substantial amounts of isopropyl alcohol. When finished, he had discarded the alcohol-soaked cotton into the wastepaper basket, which was not an uncommon practice back then.

He then moved the waste basket near the side of the machine where he was working. The repair procedure required that the machine was running, while making the adjustments. He accidentally dropped a tool that fell right across the exposed electrical connections. Sparks flew, and just like the old cartoons, one of the little balls of fire shot right into the waste basket. This ignited the

Would You Fly What You Fix?

alcohol soaked cotton and set the contents of the can on fire.

A school is the last place you want to start a fire, even accidentally. He described a scene that had him running down the long hallway with a waste can on fire, and trails of smoke filling the halls. Students and teachers were filing out as the fire alarm blasted. Then, to complete his humiliation, he had to explain to the firemen how this all happened.

He said they just shook their heads and continued with their routine.

Would You Fly What You Fix?

Chapter 6

Hammers!

Is it a hammer or a bottle opener? Why brute force might not lead to the right fix and where did the extra hardware come from?

> "For want of a nail, a shoe was lost..."
> *--Quote by Benjamin Franklin*
> *In* Poor Richard's Almanac *(1757)*

> "To a man with a hammer, every problem looks like a nail."
> *--Unknown repair specialist*

Fixing a toaster is not the same as fixing the Department of Defense mainframe computer. Few would argue that having a washing machine operate properly carries the same urgency as a new cardiac pacemaker working properly.

28

Would You Fly What You Fix?

But toasters that won't toast, washing machines that won't wash, or pacemakers that don't keep hearts beating are all problems. The fact is that not many machines are self-healing. At some point, you have to go in there and *fix* the damn things.

And when that need arises, one of the most important items any true craftsman must have in his tool kit are… well, the right tools in the tool kit.

You can open a beer bottle with a ball-peen hammer, or you can use a bottle opener. I've done it both ways, and there's no question in my mind which is more effective. A cardiac surgeon *can* crack a patient's chest with a rusty Barlow knife, but the results are far more satisfactory if she uses a sterilized surgical-grade scalpel with a No. 10 blade.

My point is that the professional True Fixers make sure they have the proper tool at hand when they approach a repair job. And it's not just to show they have better toys than the rest of us. Using the tool designed for the job at hand results in a repair that is accomplished effectively. It's also less likely to do damage. Using the right tool also indicates that they know which tool to use, and *that* is as revealing as it is profound. Having the right tools means that the tech is prepared for the job and has the tools to accomplish his task correctly.

Would You Fly What You Fix?

This brings us to the subject of... hammers.

People – okay, most of them are men-- *love* hammers. When someone says "Hand me that hammer," there's no doubt that a man is about to go to work. As with many of the pet objects to which we feel a very close attachment, men tend to give this particular tool nicknames, such as "The 32-Ounce Persuader," and we'll proudly dig them out of our toolbox at any opportunity.

This tendency, however, carries a number of clear dangers.

Now, as a tool, the hammer certainly has its place. I have many different types, and it can be both fun and personally satisfactory to bang away with them.

But one should never reach for a hammer before understanding two vital points. The first point is the consequence of its use. The second is the consequence of its *mis*use.

Personally, I have no general attitude against the application of brute force. It has its place, but not when it is used as a substitute for knowledge, expertise, and good common sense. Like all makeshift implements and techniques, in every

Would You Fly What You Fix?

aspect of life, it needs to be brought out at the proper time.

For instance, in some auto shops, I've seen our 32- Ounce Persuader come out of the tool box a lot — far more often than it should.

This is a symptom. It indicates a mindset that shows up in virtually every stage of every task undertaken by a certain type of technician. It states, loudly and emphatically, that this is the type of garage where you can expect to find your new battery cables routed improperly. The result will be an open invitation to melting the insulation when the cable wire flops against the exhaust manifold. Just reckless work habits.

When, not if, that happens, the result is an expensive short-circuit, a tow back to the repair shop, and lost time. Our newly educated, but unhappy car owner, is now on a quest to find a *different* shop.

In such garages, it's also not uncommon to find "left-over" brake hardware still in the replacement kit box—often, along with the instructions that emphasize the critical importance of utilizing all parts that are included in the kit.

It's the little things that are the most revealing — and that includes the relatively simple task of putting a nut on a bolt. Some shops seem to have an unwritten motto, "Tighten it until the threads strip, then, back it off a half turn."

Don't walk: *run* away from that shop. It's likely that this careless philosophy extends to the rest of their work ethic, too.

With a little observation, five minutes is about all that is needed for most of us to know if a true technician working on a car. My own experience showed me one of the best examples. I once watched an auto technician doing a routine brake job. He opened the new-parts box, and spent time reading instructions and scrutinizing the replacement parts. He cross-checked the parts number against the work order, and then on the shop computer. Only then did he begin the job itself. To his undying credit, I saw him compare the replacement parts to the components he removed just to be safe.

I spoke to him after the job was finished. As it turned out, despite looking the same age as my children, he was by no means a rookie. He was a seasoned veteran of the auto repair industry, had done hundreds of similar brake-replacement jobs. I have no doubt, could have rattled off the needed procedures in his sleep.

Would You Fly What You Fix?

Observing his neat and professional work habits made me sleep a lot easier that night, secure in the knowledge that whoever stepped on the pedal, the brakes were going to work.

Your customers are often watching you work, too. Show them that a skilled professional is at work who will take care of their equipment.

Chapter 7

Safety on the Job and Using the Right Tool

A routine job that didn't stay routine, and how being a pro will keep customers.

Probably the first lesson learned by any craftsman (and craftswoman) is that no single tool works for every application. A skilled professional knows the specific tool for a specific need, and uses it. Ask anyone: does one-size-fits-all really exist in the highest quality tool? Any experienced tech will tell you it doesn't.

To provide a clear example of routine repair gone wrong, here is the story of an incident I witnessed. The star of this show –as you'll see a *horror*-show—was a repair technician and co- worker we'll call Rich.

By all indications, Rich was your typical guy's-guy—the kind of guy who always had a good joke, or was ready to laugh at the stories you told. He seemed like a fun and intelligent guy, and we occasionally ate lunch together. Sometimes, if I was

Would You Fly What You Fix?

caught up on my own service calls, I'd check Central Dispatch to see if Rich needed a hand.

This time he did, and, badly, as it turned out.

When I arrived at the customer's office, there was Rich, trying, with no success, to manipulate two wrenches onto an air system valve solenoid he had removed and placed at his feet. If you're not familiar with such systems, these fittings have a tendency to corrode and lock up tight.

Now, the right tool would have been a bench vise to secure the component during the procedure– not exactly a common item to haul to an office job site. As an alternative, the procedure calls for two people, one each to finesse the two wrenches required to release the nuts.

But Rich was alone, frustrated, and all-too-ready to improvise a solo approach. Now, his wrenches were awkwardly positioned on the corroded nuts, one wrench-handle parallel to the floor, and the other raised slightly off the floor. Rich had a plan that did not consider simple applied physics. This is the kind of stuff that is supposed to be understood by those with a natural mechanical aptitude.

He put the wrenches on the nuts, but then laid the device on the floor.

Would You Fly What You Fix?

Yes, his plan was to jump, with all his might, on one of the wrenches that was not biased to the floor. In theory, this may have worked if the device was securely mounted to the floor, which was not possible. He also needed to guarantee that his foot would hit the target wrench at the correct angle. Also very difficult to achieve.

That's when applied physics took over, and the two-pound steel solenoid took wings.

I watched in awe as the solenoid took flight over the desks of astonished office workers. It careened off a coffee-service station with still-impressive force. Then, it narrowly missed what would have been a painful waist-high merger with a passing manager, before finally succumbing to Newton's Law, and rolling to a halt near my shoes.

Tools, when you have the *right* one, routine jobs stay routine. When you don't, a mutual failing of professional preparedness and attitude can result. Maybe in an airborne, two-pound steel unguided missile. In Rich's case, it could have been one that made both newspaper headlines and the personal-injury courthouse docket in the first lawsuit of its kind.

Would You Fly What You Fix?

So, how do you ensure that you (and your employees) will have the right tool, and use it? Here are two simple points to remember:

1 **Define your objectives.** The first step in selecting the right tool for the job is to identify what results and/or benefits you expect to get from the tool. Are you only looking for a tool to help you get a handle on a specific unit or component? Or, far better, are you focusing on a more comprehensive approach—preparing your toolkit and on-site replacement-parts inventory to deal with the widest possible eventualities? Understanding and documenting your objectives will enable you to narrow- down on a set of tools that can meet most logical situations encountered on the job.

2 **Anticipate your requirements.** The next step in identifying the right tool (or tools) is anticipating what tool you may need. Nobody can pack a service vehicle with every tool or replacement part available—but a proper, pre-visit diagnosis can uncover valuable information, even if it comes merely

Would You Fly What You Fix?

(2. Cont'd.) in the form of an in depth telephone conversation with the customer before you leave the shop. And, when the unexpected arises (as it will on occasion) you're in much better position to respond if you've planned a procedure that allows tools and parts to be delivered to the tech-on-site in a timely manner.

When you have the tools needed for the job, you'll save time, money and busted knuckles. In every case, the effort will yield an element of quality and professionalism that customers will notice.

Being prepared –with the right tools, and with the right service-first attitude—will allow you to treat everything you fix as an airplane in which *you* would fly.

I can't leave the topic of safety without another story. If you've heard stories about safety violations and never cringed at the possible results, this one might do it for you, because it's true.

One laborer is on one side of a wall in a house. He needs to feed a cable about 3/8" thick through the wall to the garage. There is another laborer waiting to grab the cable and pull it through. The

Would You Fly What You Fix?

hole is already drilled. Looking at the drill bit full of insulation, it's obvious that the wall is full of insulation.

Sometimes, this makes it difficult to push a wire or cable through. The fibers of the insulation can make the cable veer away from the hole on the other side. This is what these two knuckleheads were experiencing.

One of them has a great idea. He feels that if the cable were more rigid then they would plow through the insulation and straight through to the other hole. Good point. Great idea.

So he tapes a marking flag (like the ones they use to mark utilities) to the cable.

This is where it goes wrong.

He decides to ask his helper on the other side to look into the hole to see how the pointed end of the flag is progressing. Better yet he decides to plunge the steel rod back and forth through the insulation. I walked on the scene and saw what he was doing. I was able to just peer over the side of the wall and saw his assistant with his cheek up against the wall, his eye looking straight into the hole. I yelled "Stop!" and the guy pulled his face back from the wall just as the steel rod rammed through. Easily, he could have lost an eye.

Would You Fly What You Fix?

Safety Tip: Always, always ask your working partner if he is "clear."

Chapter 8

Hiring Technicians

How to find new employees? Did you say Yale or jail?

"People Are Our Most Important Product."
--General Electric Corporate Slogan of the 1960s

If you ever want to be humbled, just take on a new job—one where systems and traditions are different from those you're used to.

There are few experiences guaranteed to turn a person wise in the ways of the working world, into a mass of quivering, insecure and incompetent jelly.

You're lost until the learning curve kicks in. You're unfamiliar with company operations, procedures and traditions. You are not yet equipped to represent the company in the correct and proper way.

This is precisely the situation we drop every new employee into. Because this is so often the case,

41

Would You Fly What You Fix?

let's take a look at the single most important component in any company.

I'm speaking of the people component that every company gives lip service to – hence my use above of General Electric's corporate slogan of the '60s, *"People Are Our Most Important Product,"* to the extent that it's become a cliché. (If you don't believe me, you can visit the internet and see for yourself how many companies tout a similar slogan.)

These days, this righteous sounding phil-osophy has become somewhat flexible in actual practice. Given how hard it has become to find "a few good men" (and women) in today's labor pool, this far too often translates to: "Well, we *did* call his probation officer before we put him on the payroll."

Nevertheless, whether your prospective employee's résumé says he spent the last four years in Yale or jail, this "people component" really *is* the single most important factor in whether a business succeeds or fails. And once a business has grown beyond a one-man operation, the people component becomes far more complex.

It is involved and time-consuming, but it's a recipe that consists of recruiting, training, and then managing employees. Then, frequently re-training --

and always, always, managing them. After all that, sometimes we have to fire them and start over.

We'll deal with the managing part in a later chapter. Since it's a subject to which entire books have been dedicated, it certainly deserves at least its own chapter here in this book.

As for the finding and recruiting part, websites have replaced the newspapers, and it can be a tough situation for many employers. You draw up a list of ideal candidate qualifications, hang out the "Help Wanted" sign on the internet and often grind your teeth in frustration at the quality of your catch. When the economy is good, you have too few qualified applicants. When times are bad, there are too many responses to sort through.

Unless you're exceptionally fortunate, or pay big money, you get what's out there: someone who, for whatever reason, is frustrated at his job and looking for fresh horizons... or someone who is simply looking for a job.

Randomly, you're going to hire *someone* from this mix. Mission accomplished, position filled.

That leaves us with training, a deceptively simple word. Even if a new employee has experience in a previous occupation, few people go into a new job with the full range of skills, attitudes,

and competencies needed to adequately represent you to your customers. Some companies, in fact, prefer to hire people with *no* experience. They are betting that the bad habits, or questionable work-ethic they picked up at another company are far more difficult to change than it is to train a relative rookie how to do the job *their* way, the right way.

No matter which philosophy you prefer, it's wise to treat every newcomer to your payroll as raw clay, even if some will be more inexperienced than others. Given that, it's easy to see how a good, kind and understanding teacher might be of incalculable value. After all, isn't that the kind of work-mentor you would have appreciated when you were a new-hire?

Chapter 9

The Trainer

Finding the right trainer and how to fix a 2,000 lb. copier, one sub-system at a time.

There's an almost-extinct breed of trainer that I call "the Grandpa Teacher." The title is symbolic, and I use it to generally refer to any older, wiser person that has taught the younger ones how to fix things.

Actual apprenticeships are few and far between these days. So is the patience and time that can be spared to teach someone a craft that requires knowledge and expertise.

Enter today's "training process," where learning on the job is a central component.

Often, it's the little things that matter most in training people. If you run your own shop, you may be doing it yourself. In larger operations, even with a training school, the new-hire is usually assigned to a seasoned veteran for some period of time. In both cases, though, the training of a new hire is usually

Would You Fly What You Fix?

seen as an additional task that's been added to an already-full workload involving *your* job.

It's easy to forget just how valuable - or worthless - a trainer/teacher can be. Training may be worthless if you've chosen the wrong person as the trainer. For instance, maybe your assigned trainer was told to "just fill the new guy in," or assigned to ride with him for his first month.

Not everybody enjoys teaching. Your newly minted teacher may not have wanted that additional responsibility in the first place. Moreover, he may simply feel that he's not good at it. And he may be right.

In many cases, the trainer may have only gotten the assignment because he was the first guy you saw when you escorted the new-hire into the shop. It happens. Or maybe you made a conscious decision: Chuck has been with you for years, and you're certain that he knows the systems and components inside-out. He's the guy, no doubt about, right?

Okay, but here's one place a big problem can suddenly develop. Chuck knows his job, but that doesn't make him *a* teacher, let alone the *best* trainer you could assign to a rookie. He may simply talk too fast, assume things that "everybody already knows," or, because *he* picked up his craft quickly, he may expect unrealistic learning goals. Or, and we've all seen it happen, he might simply be a jerk, one who takes pleasure in demeaning those employees lower on the ladder.

Just as potentially damaging is the hit-and-run school of training, which, even in the best of companies, can be the rule rather than the exception.

Here's a real example, from my own days as the new guy on the job. On my first day, I reported for work in the mail room at a large credit card company. My work-station was a big machine, and I say a worker feeding in large stacks of envelopes. Then, the envelopes came out the other side, (to me), apparently unchanged.

"Take the envelopes out of the trays and put them in the left-side feeder of the machine," my trainer tells me, as I watch him actually loading the tray.

"Well, go ahead and *do* it, he said. When they come out, they'll be stacked. Put them in a new tray off to the right. Someone will come by and get them. If they don't come by, you handle it."

And off he went to his own job, satisfied that I had been fully trained in mine.

Would You Fly What You Fix?

Now, this was my first day with a big company. I wasn't yet 16 years old. I had only worked for landscape companies, most of them not much bigger than my own little mowing service that I was still running on the side.

Not far from a panic, I thought *"What the hell am I supposed to be doing here,"*

For all I knew, I was suddenly responsible for the billing process of a multi-billion dollar corporation. If I screwed up, millions of customers wouldn't get their bills, the revenue flow would screech to a halt, and the resulting bankruptcy of a Fortune-something company –and possibly a global financial collapse, would all be on *my* head.

Worse, I'd get fired, and my dad was the one who got me the job.

When the "trainer" left, I turned to another guy at the machine, and asked, "Uh… so what is it we're doing here, exactly?"

He said, "We split the tops of the envelopes open with this machine." He said this simply, which signaled his status as a veteran. "Then we take them to the workers out in the office. They open 'em and pull the checks and invoices out."

Okay! *That*, I get!

Would You Fly What You Fix?

Once the purpose of my task was explained, I immediately understood the vital steps needed for proper operation of my machine. I then knew that the envelopes needed to be neatly stacked, torn or damaged envelopes removed, and loaded correctly to minimize jams.

My first instructor gave simple directions with no insight to the process. I was missing the entire picture. My second instructor provided the necessary information to do my job. This simple guidance helped me avoid hours of machine problems and frustration. My work could now be completed properly for the next worker.

Here are a few axioms in new-employee training that I've found useful in developing the kind of employee who can turn into a valuable, long-term veteran:

1. **Train your trainers.** Professional educators go to college not only to learn the subjects they will be teaching, but how to teach. Not all companies can afford training centers and specific people to do training. But whether we like it or not, if you don't have a good trainer you

may be discouraging a perfectly good employee. Help your trainers understand the essential tasks that training requires of them. Either walk them through what you expect them to do or send them to professional seminars where training the trainers is taught.

2. **Take a "Ground Zero" approach as part of new-employee training.** Respect any previous work experience, but introduce the new hire to the job as if he or she had never touched a tool before. Hasty assumptions and oversights can dramatically affect the learning process that should be designed to introduce them to "...how we do it here."

3. **Give every new hire a reasonable time to learn.** Rome wasn't built in a day. The architects, engineers, or laborers who built it, were not trained in just a single day, either. Of course, how long the training goes on varies with the employee. At some point, you have to expect competence. Don't rush a person through the process just because your production is backed up. If you do, you

must really, really want the inevitable problems to make things worse.

4. **Encourage new employees to ask questions.** I recently asked someone to tell me about the new spin balancers now used on cars. I was given a very detailed demonstration. I cannot dispute the knowledge this person had regarding the safe and efficient operation of the machine. But I've always wanted to know how it worked. I think that gives me an edge. If I don't have that piece of information, I will find it, because it bugs me not to know, and it should bug you, too.

5. **Require continuing skills development.** Your service people must realize that they were hired and trained to have the basic skills to fundamentally understand the systems that they will be repairing.

Make it clear that they are also expected to continue to educate themselves, on their own, as their career progresses. While the experiences of daily service jobs will, yield more knowledge, this comb-ined with time on the job and awareness,

Would You Fly What You Fix?

(5. Cont'd.) will yield wisdom. The more they observe parts or systems failing, the more they will understand the need to check those assemblies for possible failures in the future. This is how you build your "wisdom base."

There is more to almost any job than people give credit, at least, if you *care* about it. This surprised me. Did you know that there is such a thing as being a certified snowplow driver? In the class where you get this certification... *math* is required!

Sure, you need to know how much melting agent is needed for "x" amount of ice or snow. That's just the starting point, though, and it should be. And I must comment: if management didn't think it was necessary to train their employees to do more than just lowering the snowplow and gunning the engine, then destroying the occasional mail box would be the least of their problems.

As in every aspect of life, the new and the different can be unsettling. Unless we're taught more than just the "what," that is, unless somebody takes the time (and the trouble) to provide the full dimensions of any job, even the most simple, most

Would You Fly What You Fix?

mundane assignment can be daunting. And tentative people seldom do good work.

For that reason alone, even basic staff training must go beyond the explanation of the "what" of any job to provide the big-picture aspect, particularly the "how" and, most definitely, the "why." No job exists in a vacuum. To do it well you must know (and teach) both the specifics of the assigned task assigned and how it fits into the larger picture.

Back in the 1970s, opening the front doors of a 2,000-pound Xerox® 7700 for the first time was an awe-inspiring experience. In many ways, this was comparable to seeing the first steam locomotive in 1830. When I was a new employee in the service division, I had a basic mechanical aptitude, some experience working on cars and other machines. I felt scarcely prepared to work on this complex, state-of-the-art technology. This was one intimidating beast of a machine!

I was taught in an excellent training program staffed by excellent educators. From them, I learned that my machine, with its mass of gears, belts, wiring, switches and connections, was *not* a single, impossibly complicated monolith machine. It was, rather, a *combination of subsystems*, each of which

Would You Fly What You Fix?

could be isolated, dissected, and reduced to a series of straightforward operations that could be analyzed, and repaired, in a logical process.

This is knowledge bred of careful training, which ultimately meets, and marries, experience. From this happy union, a new generation of competency is born.

Chapter 10

It's Not Rocket Science?

It is rocket science.

"Well, it's not rocket science."

We've all heard it said about a lot of things. We hear it over and again: "It's not rocket science." It's often the case that the overall work involved in a project seems relatively simple, but there's usually more to it. Sadly, some people in the repair industry diminish their trade by not understanding the rocket science behind their work. Manufacturers sometimes contribute to this problem by providing videos that lead the Do It Your-self crew (DIY) to believe there's nothing to it!

So, if it's not rocket science, it's a simple job, right? But it's startling to realize how many repairs are made to finished building and construction projects because of the rocket science that *wasn't* considered.

Many of these mistakes may be unchecked when a system is underground or out of sight

Would You Fly What You Fix?

behind a wall. It doesn't really take much skill to glue or clamp two pipes together. But to design the system for proper efficiencies, consider pressure losses, proper pipe sizes, and correct application of the materials *is rocket science*. These calculations are degraded when installed or repaired by technicians who are oblivious to the design and engineering of the product.

You decide to install a lawn sprinkler system. This should be a straightforward job. Dig a trench. Get some simple tools, like a shovel. Buy some pipe and assemble the system. Although many home improvement stores will design the system and do the math, many homeowners still believe it's not rocket science, and they will figure it out as they work.

I was once called to a job-site where a lawn sprinkler system had been installed and was barely functioning. My first question was what size pipe did you use? This was important for at least two reasons.

1. Water pressure at the sprinkler head is determined by pipe length, diameter and type, among other things.

Would You Fly What You Fix?

2. Pressure loss is different between copper pipe, PVC pipe, and garden hoses.

This project was installed originally with ¾ inch pipe, which was incorrect to start with. Before contacting me, the homeowner sought help from a buddy and was told that a smaller pipe would increase water pressure. He ripped out the ¾ inch pipe and installed ½ inch pipe only to compound the problem and find that the system performed even more poorly.

The friction / loss characteristics of the ½ inch pipe actually resulted in further pressure loss. It's a common myth that water pressure is increased by using smaller diameter pipes.

This will cause an increase in the velocity of the water, but it causes a pressure loss.

His system was barely working. So, this simple DIY project had to be pulled apart for the second time and re-installed with 1 inch pipe to work properly.

If the rocket science had been done, it would have been installed with 1 inch pipe the first time.

So, is it rocket science? That homeowner installed the same system three times. He used three

Would You Fly What You Fix?

times the amount of pipe necessary, and had the frustration of learning that there's more to it than putting pipe in the ground.

People are led to believe by the Do-It-Yourself marketers that many projects are for the home handyman. Many times they are, but handymen can have different levels of skill.

Take the time to understand the rocket science behind your work.

Chapter 11

Troubleshooting

Best practices for troubleshooting. How to develop thoroughness and self-discipline.

"Well, *there's* your problem."
--Phrase spoken by all service technicians, often when problem turned out to be something else entirely.

The heart of fixing any problem is to, simply enough, to identify the fault (or, more commonly, the *faults*) and to apply the proper remedy.

So far, so good, but as with any plainspoken statement, the devil is in the details.

It's important to remember that if something doesn't work as it was designed, engineered and built to work, there is a reason for it. Particularly in the area of inanimate objects, like the evil machines that often populate science fiction movies, machines simply aren't yet equipped with the self-awareness to plot a rebellion against humanity.

Would You Fly What You Fix?

Now, I've kicked my share of non-starting automobiles, smacked the sides of non-functioning televisions, and even shouted blistering curses at nuts and bolts that stubbornly refuse to loosen. It may make me feel better, but such exercises seldom bring the problem closer to a resolution.

The simple fact is that you must have an understanding of how a system or component should work, so you can understand why it is *not* working.

This principle applies whether the problem at hand is a balky car, an inoperative copier, or even a troubled marriage. It is key to a process that involves applying a logical approach to solving problems, by understanding the system or systems involved and eliminating possible reasons for failure.

We call this process "troubleshooting," and it is the defining attribute of all truly successful professionals. It requires skill and training, patience and perseverance, and a stubborn devotion to doing the job right.

On a basic level, this can be achieved by using a number of resources and best practices:

Instilling a tenacious approach to the problem's solution. This translates into an emphasis on systematic analysis, that is, one must consider more than the superficial solution when dealing with a potentially complex, interrelated problem.

Utilizing product or industry specific materials and education. Examples include repair programs taught by the manufacturer, or in the case of auto mechanics, material made available by accredited auto repair schools or the car manufacturer.

Use of documentation such as service bulletins and schematics. After having gone through formal training, a professional technician should know how to read schematic diagrams, specification charts, and understand terminology. He must be able to relate service bulletins or tech tips to products or systems serviced.

Visual, or audio observation, and physical actuation. It sounds simple: you watch systems or components *work*. An alternative may be observing an identical system or component that isn't working properly, if only to use as a reference.

A standard operating procedure of following up on *all* suspicions. It's not permissible to stop merely because the tech believes they have found the "Eureka Piece," the faulty component that, in their analysis, most likely caused the failure of the whole system. The follow-up work and continuing the troubleshooting procedures may uncover secondary, or, additional new problems.

Not surprisingly, as our list above indicates, the hallmark of professional-level troubleshooting is thoroughness.

For instance, as I mention in Chapter 13, all too often, when investigators look into reasons for failures of a complex system they look for a single, system-catastrophic "Eureka piece."

Some techs put an imaginary stop sign at some point where they feel it is ridiculous, unproductive, or simply a pain in the butt to continue troubleshooting their way through a system. They wipe their hands, close the car hood or access panel, and declare the problem solved.

But simply declaring victory and departing the battlefield seldom wins any war. And in in our example, it doesn't mean that there aren't other, contributing component failures that will return to haunt the customer (and technician).

This is why a professional, well-trained troubleshooter doesn't stop when the initial symptoms seem to have been corrected.

Would You Fly What You Fix?

I often service my own car, but when I do take it to an auto mechanic, there's a quick analysis that I've used for decades. It has its roots in those long-ago pre-computer days, when I would look for the shelf where most garages keep their repair manuals. If they were all lined in a tidy row, their covers clean and pristine, warning bells began clamoring in my head. The odds were good that they were seldom touched, let alone used, as a touchstone for the maze of complexities that constitute automotive systems.

But, if the books appeared well-thumbed, even somewhat stained, by grease-covered hands, I considered it a good sign. To me, it meant that somebody was not depending on memory or intuition, and was conscientiously applying the proper processes and cross-checks.

In today's computerized world, for just the same reason, I find myself sneaking a look at the keyboard where auto technicians call up the schematics and exploded-parts diagrams. If the keys are properly worn down, I get the same warm and fuzzy feelings that the well-used manuals once gave me.

It's by no means a guarantee of good service-- but it certainly signals to me that thoroughness is

Would You Fly What You Fix?

part of the culture in that particular garage. A good service person actually reads the instruction manual, and that is a comfort to me. This indicates a commitment to doing the real job: to solve the problem, fully and completely.

Consider the service technician who rolls into the client's facility at 4:00 on a Friday. It's the last scheduled call of the day, and our tech is anxious to start the weekend that might begin without him.

His quick visual and audio observation leads to a logical diagnosis: the main drive chain must be replaced.

Now, this is an involved procedure. It requires major component removal, inspection of other components that may also need replacement, and a trip to the service vehicle for the parts. The vehicle is parked eight stories and a parking lot away. If the service van hasn't been stocked with the right parts, there's also a possible trip back to the parts depot. The customer is a big account, and important to his company. The customer has also made it clear that they *really* need this machine to be working properly for the next shift.

Still, it is Friday afternoon. Your tech has a date, and knows he must go home, shower, change, and drive 15 miles to meet his date.

Would You Fly What You Fix?

What happens next is a product of a number of factors, most of them involving how well our technician understands choices and consequences.

A good friend, an exceptionally wise man, told me that, each day, people are faced with opportunities, choices, and consequences. Thoroughness can be taught, just as self-discipline can be developed at any time in life. The individual must recognize the need to develop these character traits. The question often becomes: How thorough do you want yourself to be?

In the example of the employee above, the choice is simple: do a proper, professional job… or choose *not* to.

If the techs choice is to not complete the job correctly, his manager may have some major troubleshooting to do. Has he failed in instilling the essential attitudes and commitment that the job demands?

In your own troubleshooting, realize that you must have much in common with any skilled investigator, for instance, a trained police detective. You, as the detective, must be as thorough as humanly possible.

To be good at this, you need to use *all* of your senses. Smell, hear, feel, see and (if appropriate and

Would You Fly What You Fix?

non-toxic) taste! A detective will want to question people that may have been close to the scene of the crime.

Look for clues. If your problem is with a copy machine, look in the waste basket for clues. If you're fixing a lawn sprinkling system, you may look for discoloration of the lawn. When working on an engine, the color of the spark plugs or the appearance of the tail pipe can give you clues.

In every police procedural show on TV, detectives are always being told to "canvass the neighborhood." You must also find customer witnesses and interview them. When does this happen? Was there a noise? What made you think there is a problem? Who else was around and noticed something?

I remember being with a seasoned service technician just after my graduation from Xerox® training classes. We were having a conversation, something totally unrelated to copy machines, while operating a machine that we just repaired.

I was in the middle of my sentence when this veteran tech put his finger in the air to quiet me.

I didn't know it, but I was about to learn something very important.

Would You Fly What You Fix?

He was obviously listening to the machine. After a moment, he pulled an access panel, made an adjustment and ... closed his eyes.

A moment later he smiled and nodded his head.

I was amazed and humbled by what I just learned. My mentor had shown me that there was not just a single instrument playing, but instead, an entire orchestra. His attention, *his thoroughness*, was focused on the larger picture of the system as a whole. By finding that final adjustment, he prevented the call-back that otherwise would have been required.

We all need to listen for the entire orchestra, to appreciate where there are harmonies. Learn to be alerted by any flat notes or missed cadences. When given the opportunity, take the time to educate your peers to do the same.

And when you do, they will hear the orchestra too.

Would You Fly What You Fix?

Chapter 12

The Pro

What makes a pro, and the consequences of "easier"

Some techs think that they "Save the day" by fixing in a pinch what should have been fixed properly in the first place. Some people run their lives in a similar way by always "Making good on their mistakes." Neither way will win points with your peers or your boss, and it can be costly.

I remember the super techs. When I started out, these guys did dirty jobs wearing white shirts and ties. Now, most of these jobs allow casual wear, and this certainly seems more practical. Any tech surely feels more ready to tackle the dirty work without staining a white shirt. Still, I've got to give credit to those guys back in the sixties and seventies for being able to do their jobs well, work around toner all day, and keep those white shirts clean. In my mind, this definitely puts those techs in the upper crust.

Would You Fly What You Fix?

The consequences of "easier." Sometimes, easier is not better. Easier can also be dangerous.

Is it ego? Is it laziness? Is just an innocent but inflated belief in ones abilities?

One of my former employee once told a story about one of his projects. He was going to take down the chimney in an old house. To make it easier, rather than working from the top down, he developed a plan. He and his assistant began beating the bricks apart at basement level. This was supposedly to cause a controlled demolition of the chimney. His calculations failed to consider the age of various fasteners that attached the chimney to the house.

Sure enough, when a few dozen bricks were knocked out, the chimney came down. It also claimed a 6-foot radius surrounding the chimney on each floor. I understand that the noise and a surrealistic filling of the basement with bricks did not match the customer's dissatisfaction. Obviously, this was not a pro at work.

What else makes a pro? Having all the right tools that will save money and yield a quality result. Customers will notice. Do not borrow the customer's tools, no matter how cold it is outside, or how far your vehicle is parked. Be prepared.

Would You Fly What You Fix?

Once, I was at a friend's auto shop after hours for a Friday night of car talk and beer. This night I would receive a special education. I got to see what a real professional in the automotive field looked like in action. He was doing an after-hours job, replacing a transmission cooler for a few extra bucks. I was watching him while he worked. Here's an outline of what I observed.

Method: disassembly, observation, verification, re-assembly, test, always exercising patience. He was also careful to read the instructions. What makes a professional? That's what makes a professional. I know a lot of guys who do car repairs on the side. Some make their living at it, others do it to save some money. Either way, this is the kind of guy that I want fixing my airplane.

A very good friend told me about his father, and how he fixed a broken side view mirror on his Volkswagen. His dad was a Russian immigrant, up in his years, but he took the time to countersink a new hole so the screw would fit properly. It didn't hold the mirror better, or improve the aerodynamics of the car. This was how he worked and how he wanted the result to look. He was a *technician*! I believe a technician is to a repairman what an educator is to a teacher, or an aviator is to a pilot.

Would You Fly What You Fix?

So what is it that makes the "Professional?" What makes the difference between a pro and one who is not?

Here's a list, and it applies for any trade:

1. **Tools.** Pros use tools that last. Tools that save time also provide the best mechanical advantage. A pro always uses tools that are appropriate for the task at hand. What will a customer think when he sees a tech using a cheap, bargain basket flat blade screwdriver to remove a Phillips head screw? What will that screw look like when you're done mutilating it? How will the next service tech be able to do his job when the screw has been stripped? This leads to another point on principles and ethics. Always think about what the next technician will have to work with on the next repair. Not only is your name on it, but as an ethical human being, you shouldn't be leaving problems that you were paid to clean up. A good example is wiring junctions and terminals. I've seen people leave wire junctions looking like a birds nest. Poor wire nut installations, and "changes" not noted in the log, mean that the next guy will have no idea of what work has

Would You Fly What You Fix?

(1. Cont'd) been completed. The condition you leave the work-site reflects back on the tech, your company, and the cost to the customer if it has repaired all over again, the correct way.

2. **Have all the tools you need** for the job. If you don't have them, go get them before you start the job. You're not MacGyver and you're not stranded on a desert island, forced to improvise with the materials at hand!

3. **Use and care of tools.** There is a right and wrong way to use channel locks, crescent wrenches, and pipe wrenches. I've seen more misuse of this group of tools than any other. Does the term "feed and speed" come to your mind when using power drills or saws? It should. Drill bits are burned and dulled by using the wrong speed when drilling. Too many drills have gone into the shop for repairs because the thrust bearings have been sent to their grave by people pushing too hard and to driving too fast into the material being drilled.

4. **I knew a guy** who prided himself on burning out two metal band saw blades in 6 hours of work. He demonstrated how he put all of his

strength and weight into pushing the saw blade into some steel bars he was cutting. I advised him that had he been working for me, I would have used all my weight and strength to push him out of my company.

It's safe to say that I believe in fixing things properly. It's not just results, it's very much about how you got those results. Watch what you do with your tools. They can get stolen, especially if you leave them on the job site. Use as many organizing accessories as you can find. These can be found at all hardware stores and anywhere else that sell tools. It's a great way to quickly check that you've got everything before you leave the job.

5. **Education in your field.** There is certainly merit in learning from talented, skilled people like your dad, or a mentor in your industry. But getting an education from a structured, industry specific class will help drive you over the top.

Remember though, there's a difference between knowledge and wisdom. Knowledge can be achieved by just about anyone who can absorb

Would You Fly What You Fix?

information from a good teacher. Wisdom, though, can only be achieved through time and experience. Wisdom is the ability to observe, retain and manipulate information into useful result. I know a young man who graduated accounting school, and then helped a friend by doing his tax return. With his new diploma and applying his new education, he proudly used every deduction he could find, remembering his professors and text books. This yielded the biggest tax return his friend ever received. It also yielded his friend's first tax audit... education vs. wisdom.

Professionals must realize that they are hired because they are thought to have the basic skills to understand the fundamentals of the systems on which they will be working. The expectation is that they will continue to educate themselves on their own, continuously, as their career progresses. It's further expected that the experiences of daily service work will develop skills and yield more knowledge. This knowledge, combined with months and years on the job, awareness, and retention, will provide wisdom. The more a technician encounters equipment failures, the more he understands the need to troubleshoot more

carefully for other, less obvious, faults. This is how you build your wisdom base.

The use of commercial grade parts and products is another key consideration. Commercial grade parts or products are those items that are built stronger and to better specifications. This may not be noticeable to a non-professional. Always look to industry codes and standards. Many people don't realize that a lot of commercial grade parts cost about the same as the "Do it yourself" parts that are found at home improvement stores

A finished product should reflect neatness, straightness, and a plumb, uniform consideration for things that the nonprofessional wouldn't notice and may not even understand.

What *are* the essential components needed to be a true professional, particularly in the eyes of those who want to hire one?

Here's a simple four-point list, which has worked well throughout my own work life, both as a services supplier and a consumer:

1. **Ability.** There's nothing better than sheer competence when it comes to demonstrating that that you are a true professional. When

(1. Cont'd.) you know the right wrench to apply to the proper nut on the correct valve that adjusts the flow to the perfect volume — well, that's when you've demonstrated that you're skill is the result of careful training, intensive experience, and profound judgment. By itself, ability, may only mark an individual as a good technician; but for anyone who aspires to be a "professional," it's an essential starting point.

2. **Responsibility.** The single most important path to success: "Show up and get to work." The consummate professional shows up at the designated time and aims to please... whether or not she (or he) feels like it.

3. **Respect.** Any professional has a deep respect for the intrinsic worth of the specialized nature of the work that he performs. Respect must also be paid to the customer for whom that work is being done. Inevitably, the work of a professional is being done in support of some larger goal. You may only be replacing a circuit board in a copier, but your customer's office is at a standstill until you finish. Respecting that overall objective is an essential part of providing value through the

services being performed.

4. **Honor.** A professional holds tightly to a strict code of ethics, whether or not that code is written or mandated by law. Surprisingly, that code often exists only in the character of the person doing the work. Acting honorably is an essential part of building a reputation and instilling a sense of trust in those to whom we provide our services. Even more importantly, it is not only a signal to our customers but also a commitment that spurs us to providing outstanding performance.

Chapter 13

Putting Up Stop Signs

How to work through imaginary stop signs by being consistent and thorough.

What would you think of a doctor who walks out of an examining room wondering, "Why didn't I take out the stethoscope and check his heart? Maybe I should have checked his blood pressure and cholesterol, too."

Good doctors have a routine, and they follow it with every patient. First, your blood pressure is taken. The stethoscope is pulled out, and he listens to your heart. There will be general questions about how you feel, followed by more specific questions about your particular condition. How long have you been feeling this way? What over-the-counter drugs have you been taking? Are you allergic to any drugs?

Technicians and other professionals can find excuses put up stop signs when doing their jobs. Is

Would You Fly What You Fix?

the job really finished, or is it "good enough?" There are consequences to this bad habit. Have you ever placed a carry-out food order, only to get home and discover that it's not what you ordered? Have you ever gotten in the car have to drive back, wait in line, have the order corrected, and then drive back home. Again. On the return trip, management made the order right, but are you really happy with this "fix"?

Have you ever sensed that your service provider is rushing or not paying attention? If so, are they really taking care of your needs? You will be looking for a new doctor if he doesn't perform the basic procedures. Good doctors, though, understand the necessity of doing the basics on every patient, every time. These fundamental assessments, and their results, provide a foundation for his diagnosis. When you leave his office, he will either know your basic condition or will know that further testing is needed for a diagnosis. Technical repairs and troubleshooting require the same discipline.

It's an individual decision to have self-discipline and to be thorough. The question

Would You Fly What You Fix?

becomes "How thorough do you want to be?" and "How thorough do you need to be?"

I believe thoroughness can be learned and taught. It's learned when the result of your lack of thoroughness causes problems. It's taught when you've practiced it and your work becomes better as a result.

When an airplane goes down, investigators look into the reasons for whole system failures; they look for the "Eureka" piece. I repeat this because the "Eureka" piece may just be another stop sign. This piece is a component that most likely contributed, in a major way, to the failure of the entire system. There may still be other component failures that contributed to the crash. This is why a troubleshooter cannot stop there. It can be exciting to find the initial fault and you will feel accomplishment. But the truth is, your work isn't finished at this point.

Verify your repairs! Think back about that doctor. Would he install that pacemaker and then not check to see if it's operating correctly? Like that doctor, the more you know, the more you will check. Experience will teach you. Things will work better because of your complete approach to the job. Oddly enough, with this thought process, repairs

Would You Fly What You Fix?

will get easier and harder at the same time. The job is because you will identify all potential faults and fix them. The job will be easier because your repairs will be high-quality and comprehensive.

A service technician that does not qualify his diagnoses or verify his repair is either lazy or arrogant. I knew a tech who thought that fixing the customer was easier than fixing the machine. He figured that instead of adjusting a guide-roller assembly, he would instead tell the customer to hold the paper slightly to the left. This would compensate for the misadjusted part. This approach works until some other company offers to sell your customer a machine that doesn't require that work-around.

Make sure your work is done right. Check out all the systems and subsystems. Don't hesitate to check other things that you know may be loose or wearing out, even though that's not what you were called out for. Use all your senses: touch, see, smell, and listen to check on assemblies.

A lack of thoroughness can lead to callbacks. Too many callbacks from too many shortcuts will lead to bigger problems, and will cause you to lose customers.

Would You Fly What You Fix?

I once heard an Army general talk about his approach to solving battlefield problems. "There are *always* problems on any battlefield. But the temptation is to look only at the 'big picture, the things that *are* happening. One should also pay attention to what's <u>not</u> happening!"

The same advice applies to technicians when troubleshooting problems with machines.

There are many ways to put up stop signs. I have seen and worked with a lot of inept repairmen. Sometimes they were paid more than me. I knew techs who would take service calls with only a Swiss army knife and a pair of channel locks. These "technicians" were convinced that they did not need to lug around a full case of tools. Can you imagine following one of these guys on a service call. Stripped screws, bent this and bent that. None of the adjustments were in specification. WD 40 was sprayed excessively and then pooled in the base of the machine. I would recognize immediately that I had to tear down all the stop signs, start from scratch, and work through all the systems to make a good repair.

Early in my career, I had a co-worker who thought it would be easy to be a good field service technician. It sounds incredible now, but the owner

Would You Fly What You Fix?

of the company hired Larry because he was a funny guy and had good customer skills.

I told the owner that Larry was a knucklehead and that he was likely to cross-thread a light bulb. He replied that his ability to amuse the customers would outweigh his technical skills. Well, he was wrong on both counts, and Larry was one of the most annoying people I ever met.

Larry's ego and arrogance caused him to put up stop signs, early and often, on all his service calls. One time he met me and a few of the other techs for lunch after one of his "quick" service calls. I already knew what the machine symptoms were before I asked him about the problem and how he had solved it. His diagnosis was 180 degrees from what I knew to be correct, and his remedy was equally off. I asked why he thought he'd solved the problem because I couldn't understand how his solution had worked. He didn't know, but the problem had gone away after he did whatever he did. This is where he put up his stop sign. And probably got out of there quick!

Sure enough, I was dispatched to the same machine later that day. Yes, I did have a logical solution that was different from his, and the

problem did not re-occur after I made the correct repair.

To be sure, I would not fly in anything that Larry said he fixed. It won't surprise you to hear that his technical career never really worked out at that company.

True and long lasting repairs don't happen by magic. There is always a reason that something is fixed. Be determined to find it. You can do it without limiting the customer's use of the equipment. The customer will have better, more reliable equipment use because of your diligent repairs.

Always be truthful with yourself; did your "fix" really solve the problem? The more times you find the answer, the closer you'll be to becoming a True Fixer!

Chapter 14

Callbacks and Disasters Part 1

How to be "The Make Sure Company" and the true test of a service organization

A "callback" in the service industry is just that: returning to a customer site for a problem that you thought was fixed, but wasn't. As a manager and owner, I look for profit and do what I can to avoid loss of that profit. I'm always concerned about callbacks because the callback contributes to lost profit, interferes with efficiency, and invites the kind of attention from your customer you don't want. Callbacks just might be at the top of a list of unwanted problems in the service industry. There are all kinds of ways to lose money in business and the callback is a obvious way to do just that.

Reliability is a product that is marketable. Your company's success and reputation depends on what your team can deliver to service calls and

customer concerns. And that means right now and on every service call! Although we can't guarantee against failure we must strive to avoid it. Perform your tasks like the customer is always watching and watch your efficiency improve.

Be "The Make Sure Company:" The callback is costly, no matter what the cause. This makes it all the more reason to practice the *"Would You Fly What You Fix"* work ethic. The front line techs, and the entire service team, must work together to reduce the possibility of a callback. Management must provide the techs with the company's philosophy, rules, procedures, and techniques that make that happen. Every manager, including the owner and senior management must carry that message to everyone below. We're talking about making sure; being the company that customers know as "The Make Sure Company."

All callbacks are not our fault. This is where customer perception trumps reality. We know that even the best performing service teams are not perfect. Sometimes our vendors fall down and don't

Would You Fly What You Fix?

deliver as promised. Parts, even the highest quality parts, can be faulty and fail an hour after installation. But try telling that to your customer now, when things are going to hell.

And then there's Murphy's Law that says that "Everything that can go wrong - does go wrong." This law isn't a myth like the Loch Ness Monster. It really happens, and usually at the worst possible moment. Your customer doesn't care why the machine is down. He doesn't care about your staffing problems. He's paying you to fix his problems, and he wants his equipment fixed, now.

The callback affects (not necessarily in this order) the service technician, the service manager, the whole technical support team, and, of course, your customer. This, in turn, will affect the short term and long term success of your company.

What are the consequences of callbacks?
- Lost profit and revenue
- Lost customer
- Loss of your good reputation
- Oddly, maybe a customer for life

Would You Fly What You Fix?

Lost Profit and Revenue: What will calm down the customer when he's the most upset? What can you do to keep the customer? Whatever you do, it's going to cost money. Sometimes giveaways are a way of calming things down. Maybe there are reduced charges, or no charges. This means more lost profit, or just loss at that point.

Lost Customer: The customer may now have lost money too. They may also have missed deadlines and now have overtime costs for their employees. The customer may now have hurt their reputation with *their* customers, and another subsequent loss of revenue and profit. The decision maker may not be defending his decision to hire you if he has failure staring him down. He may have made his own set of promises that are now in jeopardy. His boss is now asking tough questions about the quality of service and the need to start considering other vendors.

Loss of Your Good Reputation: And then there's your company. The longevity of your success and the strength to keep competition at bay

Would You Fly What You Fix?

all depends on what your company brings to the table. Remember, reliability is a product that is marketable. It should be obvious now that work must be completed properly. A customer with a poor perception of your work will cause the loss of reputation, business, profit, and jobs. Remember that bad news seems to circulate faster than good news.

Making a Loyal Customer after a Disaster. *The real measure of a service organization is how it handles difficult situations.* Life is good when everything is running well. The real test for a service company begins when everything stops running so well. The customer needs to hear that you understand and that you will do everything possible to correct their problem, and that you are working with urgency when they most need you.

Chapter 15

Callbacks and Disasters, Part 2

The real test of a service organization is how it responds to difficult situations.

How Good Can You Make the Repair? Knowing that callbacks are the number one enemy, techs must not ask how good the repair has to be but how good it can be made. A balance of skill, technique, and experience provides better repairs. Imagine digging someone out of an avalanche with a sharp shovel. Certainly speed is important. But, if working recklessly, you hit the person with your shovel... Well, I think you get the point...Or the guy under the snow certainly does.

Would you fly what you fix? All of the correct approaches of working in the WYFWYF mode reduce the possibility of the call back. Reduce call backs and you will reduce the loss of customers and

Would You Fly What You Fix?

the loss of dollars. You will also maintain your reputation as a quality service provider. The proper handling of the customer and the situational awareness practiced on each call reduces the possibility of a call back.

So, what do you do when the day falls apart in the service business? More importantly, how can it be re-assembled and put back together. Here's what I've seen played out more than once in the service business.

The Technician: Bob has a callback to confront the same problem on the same piece of equipment. First, he must face the customer again, wondering if they will maintain their confidence in his ability to solve the problem. Bob also knows that his service manager isn't going to be happy. There is already has another customer waiting for him and now they're being pushed back on the schedule. Bob knows that these incidents may affect his performance review, and he may begin to doubt his own abilities, just when confidence in front of the

customer is most needed.

The Service Manager: Because of the callback, I know that other customers are waiting and my response time has been compromised. Depending on the nature of this callback, the ranking of the customer, and how upset they are, I have to start considering my options. Other work must be rescheduled, maybe a lot of other work. Decisions are now going to be revolving around this problem, taking focus away from other priorities. Calls must made to other departments, including sales and dispatch. Let's hope there's not an installation scheduled for a new customer. The costs are adding up.

In a tough situation, the customer may request (or demand) another technician who "knows what he's doing." This is bad for any technician. If too many accounts don't want him, he can't generate revenue, and then even tougher decisions need to be made.

The Customer: His equipment is still down. They may be losing money and favor with their

Would You Fly What You Fix?

customers because of a deadline that will be missed. They have this problem because we didn't fix things correctly the first time. They want it fixed, now. They want to know your plan and timeline to make it right.

Fixing the Problem and the Customer: The customer needs to hear that we are focused and working on his repair. He needs to know that we care about this issue and are doing everything possible to correct the problem. I call and explain that I understand the urgency, and that I will dedicate every resource to solve this.

Listening to the Customer: This is a critical piece. Listen to your upset customer and give him a chance to vent his anger. Tempers may be flaring and the customer may take out his problems on the technician, service manager and anyone else in his path.

The customer needs to see composed, confident professionals at work. State your position calmly and briefly: "I'm working on the problem and will have it fixed as soon as possible. I

understand you need your equipment up and running and I'm doing everything I can to fix your machine."

Identify needs to make this repair as quickly as possible. All resources available to you must be considered. What parts are needed? Can an entire assembly be replaced to reduce labor time? Be prepared to send your best tech out to help close out this call.

Set clear goals for the technicians. Tell them what needs to happen and how it will happen. They should understand that parts are available and being delivered. A tech specialist is available for phone calls, or onsite if needed. It is essential that the onsite tech communicate with me about any other needs that develop. Keep the customer informed about our plans to fix the problem.

After the crisis is over, meet with the customer. This is not the time to avoid a conversation. There has been a major problem and the customer may be ready to replace you with another vendor.

Would You Fly What You Fix?

Identify the personnel that should be there, and be ready for tough questions and comments. Bring one or two team members along, but choose them carefully. Do not march in with five or ten people. This will cause a loss of focus, and irritate the customer. Have a discussion before the customer appointment to clarify roles. Every team member should know his role and speak to only the points necessary.

Let the customer lead. Your customer will have no trouble starting this discussion and he may have a lot to say. Much of it will be uncomfortable, but hear them out and do not interrupt. Letting the customer unload their frustrations is one reason for this meeting. They need to know that you hear them, understand their problems, and will continue to do everything to avoid this problem from happening again. Are they aware of the resources you deployed to resolve the emergency? Ask them what could have done better.

Would You Fly What You Fix?

Review the steps:

1. Set a customer meeting.
2. Let the customer vent any residual anger
3. Express concern for customer problems
4. Review the event and outline the actions that were taken
5. Could more have been done?
6. Discuss your commitment to reliability and quality
7. **Explain:** The real test of a service organization is how it handles difficult situations.
8. **Review your actions.**
   a) Commitment of necessary resources
   b) Commitment to resolve issues
   c) Commitment to customer satisfaction
   d) Service company stepped up when the chips were down
   e) Did not quit until the problem was resolved

Would You Fly What You Fix?

Would you fly what you just fixed? The future of the company and the employees are the stakes here. It's important that technicians work with this in mind. Always ask why your repair solved the problem. If you don't have a sound reason, then you probably didn't really fix it. The better technicians will be able to say with certainty why their solution fixed the problem.

Technicians cannot guarantee against a particular failure. Each day, though, the mission of the company must be to reduce the possibility of downtime for every customer. This is accomplished by having the entire service team understand the mission, procedures, and techniques that contribute to reliability. Once again, we're talking about making sure the problem is solved, right?

Chapter 16

Thinking About the Jerry Rig

Real world decisions, the temporary quick fix and never jeopardizing safety

I've spent a lot of time talking about how to do things right. Taking extra steps to make sure repairs are made complete is always important.

Now, I'm about to tell you that there are exceptions to every rule. Because I'm in the real world of fixing things, there are times when a temporary fix might be made. I understand that something repairs to be done with a particular and careful approach. I also know that, sometimes, circumstances won't allow it.

About the jerry rig: It's one of those terms everyone knows, and often has awful implications. Basically, it's a temporary quick fix, and that's what I'm discussing here. I don't think there can be a digital, on-off sort of rule about deciding to make a jerry-rig fix. This fix is used in a stressful, time-sensitive situation. The jerry-rig is in a gray area of judgement, and there is a lot of responsibility that

Would You Fly What You Fix?

comes with making this decision. When should the decision be mad to jerry-rig?

These are some considerations to make when that time comes. First, how much time you have to make the equipment operational again. Second, the urgency of the customer's demands will be one guide to this decision.

The customer's need, current workload, and the nature of the problem are all involved. Consider that the customer's needs might have to be delayed. You cannot bypass a fuse to get quickly bring equipment up and running again because of the danger involved.

The current service workload might be considered because it affects customer satisfaction and service team morale. Management, using their metrics, might decide that a "quick fix" should be deployed. The important word here is "might."

A temporary quick fix cannot be a dangerous fix. The immediate dynamic of the problem is this: Is something on fire or will more damage be done if a quick fix is not made? Common sense and company policy are going to work hand-in-hand with the expertise of the technician to make a correct decision. Equally important is how the repairs are made in this quick fix mode. It must last

Would You Fly What You Fix?

as long as needed, until you can get back there to make it right.

There are service technicians out there who thrive on the "quick fix". These techs seem to find a personal challenge, sometimes even going out of their way to make a patch. There's a time to be proud of making things work with very little available to you. This must always be considered temporary. If you have the ability to fix things properly, then do it. Don't let your ego get in the way.

Let's be clear that it's good to have the knowledge and skill set to improvise a fix in really lousy situations. We all hope to be that innovator when we are in a tight spot. It's just not the way to do repairs every day.

Again, the quick fix is not something you practice on every service call. Most senior technicians have been around long enough to recognize quick-fix artists. Their territories are filled with jerry-rigs and compensating tolerances. These machines usually feature more down-time and irritated customers. Eventually, that machine will need major renovations or replacement. The customer may have good reasons to pursue another vendor. If you're going to deliver a quality repair

Would You Fly What You Fix?

you don't want your name be synonymous with "the quick fix" or the "jerry rig".

Even more important than making the jerry rig fix, is getting back to that make the repair correctly with the time, material and talent to make it right again.

Chapter 17

Opening and Closing Service Calls for a Billionaire (and everyone else)

Another story from the field and how to earn a customer for life.

Opening and closing service calls may seem like the most basic of topics, not worth a chapter of discussion. In practice, though, it is an essential part of an effective service strategy. The field service technician serves as the face of the company in customer accounts. The impression he or she creates will become the perception of the service company for your customer.

The tech must be able to communicate clearly with the customer. First, the tech must understand the true nature of the service problem. This will help focus attention on the proper system or sub-system that needs correction. Second, after the problem has been corrected, the tech must be able to discuss the problem briefly, in terms the customer can understand, and demonstrate that the problem

Would You Fly What You Fix?

has been corrected. Customers notice when they are in the care of a pro.

I was early in my career at Xerox® in the mid-70s. Those of us who fixed machines in the field were called "technical representatives". The product line that I serviced was called a "duplicator." This designation was for machines that were made for large volumes of copying at the fastest speeds of the era. This equipment was intended for a customer with a lot of copying and tight deadlines. Insurance companies, utility companies, and large law firms were just some of those clients.

I received a call from new customer that had recently been added to my territory. Walking up to the reception desk at the office I identified myself to the receptionist and she called for the "key operator". I was probably all of 20 years old. After I identified myself to the receptionist, I was referred to the key operator. This was an employee designated to monitor any problems with the duplicator and place a service call when needed.

Two problems quickly became obvious: First, this client had a lot of copies to run, and, second, they perceived the machine to be unreliable.

Would You Fly What You Fix?

I asked a lot of questions about the types of problems they were experiencing and I listened to their answers. I told the key operator that I understood their situation and being the tech newly assigned to servicing their account, I going to do my best to change their opinion of that machine.

I spent the next couple of hours troubleshooting their machine as thoroughly as I could. Bear in mind, that having been on the job about three years, it was likely that I had taken well over 2500 service calls in my (relatively) newfound career.

I found problems. I made adjustments, I cleaned and replaced parts. I thoroughly tested the machine. I called the key operator over and told her that if she brought the work she needed to complete, I would wait and watch as the machine worked. If there were any magical moments to happen among those gears I was going to be there to hear it, see it, and fix it immediately. She got through her project, without incident from the machine. She was pleased, and so was I.

She seemed surprised when I asked to speak to the highest level manager in the office to discuss my work and what I did to make their machine

Would You Fly What You Fix?

reliable. My goal was to convince that person that I was genuinely concerned about turning around their opinion of that machine. As it turned out, the company was Pritzker & Pritzker, one of the world's most successful business families.

A few moments later, I found myself in Mr. Pritzker's office. I must admit I didn't know who he was or his position in the business community. I did know his name was on the front door of the office, and that told me he was probably the right person to talk to.

Using my best customer management skills, I went on to describe my work. I had found problems, I had solved those problems, and I wanted his machine to work reliably. I handed him my card, and told him that I was his new technician, that I was there to help, and that he should call me directly if there were any problems. I didn't take up much of his time. I didn't use technical terms that would have been meaningless to him. I knew he had a company to run.

We shook hands, I left his office, and went back to double-check my work on his machine, just to make sure it was still chugging along. It was working flawlessly.

Would You Fly What You Fix?

A few hours later I got a call from my manager, whose first words were "What the hell have you been doing?" I asked, nervously, "What do you mean?" He chuckled, and said "I just got a call from Rochester, New York. I was told that they just got a call from Mr. Pritzker complimenting your work." Rochester was our headquarters. I don't remember the name of the manager in Rochester, nor do I exactly remember the additional compliments offered by my manager, but I do remember Mr. Pritzker.

I also remember receiving the "technician of the quarter" award just a few weeks later.

There are basic components to doing a proper service call. In simple terms, you open, perform, and close the service call. Each company is going to have its own way of dispatching technicians to the service call. We're going to start from the point of arrival. Although I'm about to describe a procedure, I will be interjecting stories and important considerations. To make things simple, we're going to talk about two different types of customers. One is going to be the business customer service call, and the other is going to be a

Would You Fly What You Fix?

residential service call. Both cases involve common courtesies that should always be observed.

Immediately, we can see that opening the service call is different for each type. In a business setting, you may find yourself talking first with the receptionist.

Believe it or not, I find that the residential call is a little more involved. I say this is because the business situation has understood and accepted methods of first contact. A residential call means you're walking into somebody's personal space, their home. Considerations as simple as not parking in the driveway are important at a private residence.

Common sense should dictate that you don't park in the president's personal parking space on a business call. Parking in front of the loading dock and block deliveries is also considered bad form. But when working at a home, a different psychology must be understood.

Let's start with the homeowner call. The first thing we need to do when arriving is to identify ourselves and perhaps remind them why we're here. Remember, they may not have placed the service call, or forgotten that you were coming. In this case, looking the part may be an important part

of being professional. A polo shirt or jacket with the company logo will help the customer to identify you as a company representative for the customer.

Because you are entering their personal space, respect for their space and property are going to be a priority. Unlike a business, there's no security guard, and you're in someone's home, so make every effort to be noticed and visible.

Addressing the customer with a simple greeting like "Good morning, I'm Bob from ABC Plumbing. I'm here to repair the water heater" is a good way to start. A genuine smile always goes a long way in making someone feel more comfortable with you. At this point you're likely to be invited into their space.

You should already have their name. There is more than one way to deal with something as simple as calling them by their name. Based on my observations, the discussion between you and the customer begins with how you address them. If you use ma'am or sir, you're certainly being polite, but it can create a distance between you and the customer.

We typically hear military people and police regularly address people as ma'am or sir. In the first case, it's a matter of showing respect, and in the second case, it shows respect and purposely creates a distance between you and them.

I'm aware that in some parts of the United States that using ma'am and sir are commonly accepted. I think starting out with Mr. Smith or Mrs. Jones is the best way to start. I have found that customers will have a tendency to either ask you to call them by their first name or they'll just leave it alone.

You might think that I'm making too much of this, but the best situation is to have the customer feel like they know you just a bit. And notice I'm saying a little bit. I'm not talking about becoming best friends. You don't need to share your life story with them, but it makes it easier to become repeat customers when they find a company with somebody they already know and like. If a proper rapport is built between the service technician and the customer that relationship will extend to your company, too. Instead of "The plumber was out today," it will be "Bob was here from ABC Plumbing". When customers know their technician by the first name, they're indicating that you're a notch above a strictly business relationship.

After introductions, ask pertinent questions regarding their problem. Do not discuss the Ferrari in the garage. It will either make them think that you are going to overcharge them, or just give them a unsettled feeling of noticing too much about their personal property. Remember, these aren't your friends, and they're meeting you for the first time. Also remember that you're making a first impression and how they will come to regard you as a professional.

Consider any safety concerns. For example, is it dangerous to have children observe your work? Politely discuss any such concerns with the customer. If you don't like dogs, if possible, try not to show it. Most people will ask if you have a concern and try to put you at ease. On the other hand, if you like dogs, ask before you pet their dog. People enjoy it when you like their animals, but they may warn you against it, too.

Now we move to the second phase of the complete service call; actually performing the service call. As we talked about in earlier chapters, being professional and thorough on the job are at the front and center here. Every repair you make, no matter how small, needs to be checked for proper operation. Always remember that we don't want the customer to call back because the problem recurred.

Would You Fly What You Fix?

Respect customer property, both natural and man-made. If you discover a bird's nest in someone's yard, don't treat it as if it was a hornet's nest. Discovering newborn rabbits and showing it to your customer is a good start in building that relationship. They're learning that you both appreciate the same things. Pay attention to what you're doing. Work carefully, not just because you want to perform your repair properly, but also to avoid even minor accidents in front of them. A small cut and blood on their basement floor is not the way to be remembered. If you're careless with yourself, you might not be careful in their home. Customers don't want to worry about legal actions, even if you are bonded and insured.

Make notes of any potential problems you discover when troubleshooting. Compile the information before you go to the customer with it. Don't approach the customer repeatedly with different observations. Get it all together and approach them once with your diagnosis of the problem. Remember, there's nothing wrong with advising your customer of additional problems that may add to the scope of the work.

There are two obvious benefits. First, you are indicating that you do thorough work and are

looking out for their best interests. This also has the added benefit of generating additional, honest revenue. As you're completing your work, consider the serviceability of that work. Put tags, labels, or in some way indicate to future technicians that an upgrade has been performed.

Take a step back and ask yourself, "How easy would it be for another technician to follow you and your work?" You should also indicate things that are unique to the system and your repair. For instance, if a green wire is typically located on a particular terminal, but in this case a white wire is now in place, make a note of it. If you can fix it easily, do it. Advise the customer of this so they know you saw an irregularity and corrected it.

The customer should know that a true professional was working for them. They will know this because you were thorough, you communicated clearly, and you resolved their problem. They will understand the repairs that were made and will feel confident that their home system is working as it should.

Now you're ready for the final aspect of the service call which is closing the call.

Would You Fly What You Fix?

If the customer is available, now is the time to show them the repairs you've done. It's a good idea make sure that your demonstration will go smoothly before you ask them to see it. Consider the terminology you'll use when discussing the parts you've replaced or repaired. Your understanding of the customer's technical level and desire to understand will guide your decision.

The service industry is riddled with acronyms. If you changed out a low pressure switch, most customers are not going to know what you mean by telling them you replaced the LPS. Some customers won't care what switch was changed, they just want to know the system is working again. Then again, you may run into a customer who will be very interested in the technology, the reason for failure, and how you made the fix. I prefer to use the word "device" to describe most technical sounding components. A more common component, like a pump is likely understood, so you wouldn't call that a "device". The customer won't feel uncomfortable with your explanation and you won't sound like you're talking down to them. Start with a simple explanation and answer questions when the customer wants more information.

Would You Fly What You Fix?

So, we're closing our service call with the homeowner. This is the time to ask for payment. Asking for payment can be uncomfortable, but if you've communicated with the customer throughout the process, he will already know what the charges will be. Small talk can soften an uncomfortable moment. Remember, avoid politics and religion. Don't discuss your competition in an unprofessional way and never offer criticism of your company. Telling jokes is not a good idea either. Jokes and off-handed comments might be perceived the wrong way.

Make sure all of the charges are understood and explain any warranty for the repair. Make sure they have your business card so they can contact you with any questions. And, they can also pass your information along to another homeowner that needs a technician.

Would You Fly What You Fix?

Now let's look at the business service call.

Well, the main points stay pretty much the same. Open the call, perform the service, and close the call. But you're going to see that in doing those basic steps, there are, in fact, differences between the two types of customers. Besides identifying yourself to a receptionist or some security people, your first mission in the business world is to find the user contact.

The size of the organization is often going to dictate how many different people are responsible for different things. If you're there to fix a copy machine you need to find out who placed a service call and then why. On this call we all have our "business hats" on. You probably won't have to be concerned about children's or dogs, but, you may have to be concerned with OSHA safety regulations.

Remember, consider your customer's ability to have the rest of the company functioning normally while you fix their equipment. In a commercial environment, your actions may be noted by some, but, generally you'll be left alone to do your job.

Be aware of the likelihood that your actions will be viewed. I had a technician friend who

Would You Fly What You Fix?

worked on my service team several years ago, repairing copiers. Our service manager called him because a customer complained he was reading the newspaper instead of fixing their dead copier. As it turned out, he had been doing his job, tracking down a fault by reading electrical schematics! Now, I know that techs are using their laptops for diagnostics today, but the point is that customers can misunderstand your actions, even when you are doing your job.

Addressing your customer is usually easier than the first meeting of the homeowner. I've found that the business world doesn't have the issue of using sir or ma'am. The last time that Mr. and Ms. were regularly used was back in the more formal 1960s or 70s. Most people in all trades and levels of management seem to accept being addressed by their first name. The introduction will include first and last names and steer you in the right direction. Usually your contact will say "Hi, I'm Bill Smith" and you're response is simply "Hi Bill, I'm Chuck Davis." But look and listen for more formal environments. If the administrator to a high level manager introduces him or her as Mr. or Ms., then you should follow their lead and use the more formal greeting.

Would You Fly What You Fix?

Doing the job doesn't change. This is the performance part of the service call where you troubleshoot and repair the equipment. Closing the service call in the business world can be less casual than in the homeowner market. But, it may be even more critical that the system you have just repaired is shown to be operational again.

Because business dollars and people's jobs and responsibilities are noticed, explanations for downtime may be necessary. Understand that different levels of management must understand that their decision to use your product and service was, and still is, a good one.

Other than the differences I've just discussed, the basic anatomy of a service call stays consistent from one type of customer to another for the most part. In my experience there is a fascinating difference in how we interact with customers in their homes, with their family and how we deal with that same person when he or she is in the workplace.

I've worked both residential and business customers over the last 40 years. I've had accounts for three family generations of the homeowner type customer. I can't say the same about my corporate

Would You Fly What You Fix?

accounts. I've seen husbands and wives argue, and get divorced. Sometimes, that anxiety has affected my ability to get payment. I've been there, up close, watching the emotional effects of my customers when they've learned they just lost a loved one.

This may be a question for a psychology professor, but over my same forty-plus years of time in the field service business, I can't recall relating on quite that level in the business market.

We are taught that as professionals, our personal problems should not be part of our interaction with those around us. The message to you is, be ready to switch gears and adjust to the moment. Remember that the basics are similar. Adapt accordingly and your ability to service any type of customer will broaden.

Would You Fly What You Fix?

Afterword

Where do I fit in this?

The "Would You Fly What You Fix" story has been a vital concern for me since I can remember. It is often said about some businesses, that the grandfather started and built the business, the son grew the business, and the grandson let it go to hell.

Of course, this isn't always true, but there is enough truth to it that it's a common story. This conveys that people do amazing things because they often realize they have no choice but to succeed. When a safety net is introduced, the perceived need for perfection may be diminished. To continue the analogy, the grandson may have let the business go to hell because he simply didn't realize the efforts that were made to hand the business down to him.

When the resources aren't available, survivors learn to make do with what they have. They find strength they didn't know they had.

Growing up in the Midwest, even without a garage and the money for the best tools, I still found a way make my dad's car work. When I wanted my

Would You Fly What You Fix?

own a car, I took advantage of a repair project that was incomplete. Someone's inability to make the repair themselves, meant that I found an opportunity. So I sat in the snow, in the cold and made the repair with the tools I had available. I date myself by using these dollar figures, but I bought the car for $15, and repair parts cost me eight dollars. I drove it for two months and sold it for $250.

In the early days of my first business, I serviced an account that was 80 miles from my house. I knew that I couldn't go out there and make just a cursory inspection of the machine. I knew my repairs had to be long-lasting because I couldn't afford to go back for warranty work. That simply would have cost too much money and time.

I realized that I possessed simple qualities that allowed me the best shot at success. I've always had a fascination with how and why things work. Whether it was a secondhand bicycle or a 2,000 pound Xerox® duplicating machine, I wanted to know why there were failures. Situational awareness always helped me in this quest.

Paying attention to the unusual gave me the pathway that lead to solutions. A good test of my situational awareness came when I finally realized

Would You Fly What You Fix?

my dream of racing cars. Ever since I could read or watch TV, I soaked up as much as I could on the subject of race cars.

In my early 20s, I was lucky enough to stumble onto a mentor in that field. There I was, on a hot stretch of asphalt with 23 other cars, all of us trying to go faster than each other without killing ourselves. You learn quickly that you don't fool around in these situations.

Mistakes can be costly. Later that day I had heard about a car coming back into the pits with the driver frantically pointing to the engine bay. His crew chief opened the hood only to find that one of the mechanics had left a rag in the engine compartment that was sucked into one of the carburetors. I didn't know it at the time, but that was one of my first lessons in asking "would you fly what you fix?"

A guideline that I practice in my business ventures is the use of the Golden Rule. The simplicity of that rule allows you to practice it in almost any aspect of business. Examples are many: Do you like waiting around all day for a scheduled service in your home only to find out at the end of the day that the service company won't make it? Do you like it when a warranty that you paid for will not be honored because of a technicality in the warranty? Do you appreciate someone treating you as incompetent or inferior? Are you happy to discover that a marketing strategy was misleading? Simply stated, nobody likes or appreciates poor service and deceptive practices.

What are the ideals that explain my inherent love for fixing things? The challenge and reward for solving problems is one. Another is the acknowledgement from the customer that I've done a completely thorough and good job. Being free to go on to that next service call, without being micro-managed has always motivated me, too. These are the things that help me find gratification in the job. There is also the unexplainable appreciation for machinery of all types, old and new, and under-standing how they work. Let's face it, every day at work isn't a great day, because, after all, it is a job. But what a job!

Mark Dzierzbicki